565
Reasons to be Happy

Happy 10th Birthday, Dad

Love Shannon, Shane, Hanna & Carmen

365
Reasons to
be Happy

Magpie Books, London

Constable & Robinson Ltd
3 The Lanchesters
162 Fulham Palace Road
London W6 9ER
www.constablerobinson.com

This edition published by Magpie Books,
an imprint of Constable & Robinson Ltd 2005

ISBN 1 84529 194 8

Compiled by Diane Law

A copy of the British Library Cataloguing in
Publications Data is available from the British Library

Printed and bound in the EU

1

Happiness can come from simple and
natural things: mists over meadows,
sunlight on leaves, the path of the moon
over the water.

2

Rainbows can be found in the strangest of places. Even spilled petrol makes a beautiful swirl of colour in the puddles left behind.

❖ ❖ ❖

3

Even tiresome things can be enjoyable if you look at them right. Getting caught in a rainstorm gives you wet shoes, but also the chance to watch the complex pattern of perfect circles that raindrops spread across the puddles. You can change your shoes when you get home, but you'd never see the beauty of the water if you stayed inside.

❖ ❖ ❖

4

There are only two ways to live your life.
One is as though nothing is a miracle.
The other is as though everything is.
I believe in the latter.

Albert Einstein, 1879–1955

❖ ❖ ❖

5

Reflect upon your present blessings,
of which every man has plenty;
not on your past misfortunes,
of which all men have some.

Charles Dickens, 1812–70

❖ ❖ ❖

6

Once you really start paying attention to
the information your senses bring you, the
world is full of possibility and variety.
Not even two glasses of water taste
exactly the same.

❖ ❖ ❖

Simple things in nature can produce
enchanting beauty. If you cut an apple in
half horizontally, there's a perfect star
at its centre.

❖ ❖ ❖

A thing of beauty is a joy forever:
It's loveliness increases; it will never
Pass into nothingness.

John Keats, 1795–1821

❖ ❖ ❖

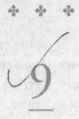

Take a music bath once or twice a week
for a few seasons, and you will find
that it is to the soul what the water bath
is to the body.

Oliver Wendell Holmes, 1809–94

❖ ❖ ❖

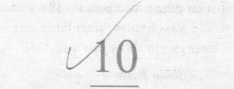

10

Happiness is something you create for yourself; it can't be handed to you in a box. Creating happiness will bring joy and pleasure for yourself and those close to you.

11

Use what talents you possess. The woods would be very silent if no birds sang there except those that sang best.

William Blake, 1757–1827

❖ ❖ ❖

12

There can be delight in the midst of a thunderstorm if you see the wonder of the energy created by nature.

❖ ❖ ❖

13

A pile of stones can become a garden with
the right amount of care.

❖ ❖ ❖

14

All beliefs are beliefs in possibilities of
some kind. Your negative beliefs, which
restrict you, are based on the possibilities
of negative things happening. Conversely,
your positive beliefs widen your experience
and are based on the belief that positive
things may happen. When you have
positive beliefs you put yourself into more
happy situations because you have a
broader outlook.

❖ ❖ ❖

15

Think of the delicate colour and texture of
a garden of flowers, the velvety surface of
rose petals and their immediately
recognizable scent. Wherever you are and
whatever you're doing you can be
transported back to a perfect
summer's day.

❖ ❖ ❖

16

You can search the world for happiness
but you won't find it. Happiness is the
way you travel not a destination.

❖ ❖ ❖

17

Life reaches out wherever you look.
The dullest sidewalk can have grass and
flowers growing in its cracks.

❖ ❖ ❖

18

You won't be happy with more until
you're happy with what you've got.

Anon

❖ ❖ ❖

19

When you're wound up generally, you're thinking of the negative things that could happen. For example, if you're scared of flying you're thinking of the possibility of crashing; the happy relaxed people on the plane are thinking of the possibility of landing and having a good holiday.

❖ ❖ ❖

20

Any small act of kindness towards
others might not see results immediately
but from one small act the happiness
can grow.

❖ ❖ ❖

21

Trouble is only opportunity in
work clothes.

Henry J. Kaiser, 1882–1967

❖ ❖ ❖

22

Action seems to follow feeling, but really
action and feeling go together; and by
regulating the action, which is under the
more direct control of the will, we can
indirectly regulate the feeling, which is
not. Thus, the sovereign voluntary
path to cheerfulness, if your cheerfulness
be lost, is to sit up cheerfully and to
act and speak as if cheerfulness were
already there.

William James, 1842–1910

❖   ❖   ❖

23

Bring your focus of attention into the
present moment. Use all your senses to get
the greatest benefit from each moment
and be thankful for the good aspects of
everything you experience.

❖ ❖ ❖

24

As soon as we see the good in something,
all the negative aspects fade and we are left
with a good feeling which makes us happy.

❖ ❖ ❖

25

Always remember things that make you
feel happy. For example, think of a
beautiful sunset or view and keep with you
enjoyable experiences of any kind.

✤   ✤   ✤

26

The smell and sound of a bonfire on a cold winter's day is always so warming to the heart. It brings to mind roasted chestnuts and mulled wine.

❖ ❖ ❖

27

Picking ripe fruit in late summer before taking it home to eat can be a wonderful way to spend a happy day.

❖ ❖ ❖

28

Be confident in who you really are and
happiness will follow.

29

Those who bring sunshine into the lives of
others cannot keep it from themselves.

J. M. Barrie, 1860–1937

❖ ❖ ❖

30

If you try to make every day a significant
day you are on the way to a happy life.

❖ ❖ ❖

31

Trying to understand people is a path to happiness. Thinking kindly of other people will make your outlook more positive and lead to you being happier.

❖   ❖   ❖

32

Think back to your childhood. Remember
the unbounded excitement that you had
about all of life at that time, believing
anything was possible?

❖ ❖ ❖

33

When you take a shower, close your eyes
and see the water as light, washing away
all the dark mist of negativity. You can
step out free of past unhappiness,
ready for future happiness.

❖ ❖ ❖

34

There will always be something good you
can accomplish, however small.

❖ ❖ ❖

35

Listen to the Exhortation of the Dawn!
Look to this Day!
For it is Life, the very Life of Life.
In its brief course lie all the
Verities and Realities of your Existence.
The Bliss of Growth,
The Glory of Action,
The Splendor of Beauty;
For Yesterday is but a Dream,
And Tomorrow is only a Vision;
But Today well lived makes
Every Yesterday a Dream of Happiness,
And every Tomorrow a Vision of Hope.
Look well therefore to this Day!
Such is the Salutation of the Dawn!

Kalidasa, c. AD 353–420

❖　❖　❖

36

Think of the surprise on someone's face when you give them an unexpected gift.

37

Lie in long grass and listen to the sound of bees and grasshoppers and you cannot fail to be cheered by them.

❖ ❖ ❖

38

Health is the greatest gift, contentment the greatest wealth, faithfulness the best relationship.

Buddha, c. 400 BC

❖ ❖ ❖

39

There is always room in life for a little bit of praise or a compliment. They can bring such happiness.

❖ ❖ ❖

40

Whoever is happy will make others
happy, too.

Mark Twain, 1835–1910

❖ ❖ ❖

41

Think of a sincere smile meant just for
you – and you'll smile to yourself.

❖ ❖ ❖

42

If you live your life in the company of
family and good friends you have the
ingredients for happiness.

❖ ❖ ❖

43

Discovering aspects of someone that you never knew existed can make you happy.

❖ ❖ ❖

44

A new friend is like new wine; when it has aged you will drink it with pleasure.

Apocrypha Ecclesiasticus 9:10

✤　✤　✤

45

The devotion of a household pet can brighten everyday life.

✤　✤　✤

46

A pessimist sees the difficulty in every
opportunity; an optimist sees the
opportunity in every difficulty.

Sir Winston Churchill, 1874–1965

47

Make room in your life for friends and
family for these are the best sources
of happiness.

❖ ❖ ❖

48

Stay, stay at home,
my heart, and rest;
Home–keeping hearts
Are happiest.

Henry Wadsworth Longfellow, 1807–82

❖ ❖ ❖

49

Become more accepting of yourself and
others and all around you will benefit
from happiness.

❖ ❖ ❖

50

The true way to render ourselves happy
is to love our work and find in it
our pleasure.

Francoise de Motteville, c. 1621–89

❖ ❖ ❖

51

Share your feelings with others. This can
make you happier than if you bottle up all
your troubles inside you.

52

There is always something new to learn:
"Somewhere something incredible is
waiting to be known."

Blaise Pascal, 1623–62

❖   ❖   ❖

53

The smell of tomatoes freshly picked from
the stem is a deliciously happy one.

❖ ❖ ❖

54

I shall never be so happy as when I was
not worth a farthing.

Alexander Selkirk, 1676–1721

❖ ❖ ❖

55

The crackle of a real fire blazing in the
grate on a cold winter's day will make you
want to curl up in its comfort.

❖   ❖   ❖

56

Seeing a matinee film on a weekday
afternoon can be a secret stolen pleasure.

❖ ❖ ❖

57

When work is a pleasure, life is a joy!
Maxim Gorky, 1868–1936

❖ ❖ ❖

58

Think of the rich colours of autumn
when the bricks and concrete around you
become too drab.

❖   ❖   ❖

59

Action may not always bring happiness,
but there is no happiness without action.

Benjamin Disraeli, 1804–81

60

The sound of falling snow can bring the
most happy and serene feelings you will
ever know.

61

When you look up at the sky, you have a
feeling of unity, which delights you and
makes you giddy.

Ferdinand Hodler, 1853–1918

62

The sun will always shine eventually even
after the most miserable of rainstorms.

❖ ❖ ❖

63

You can choose happiness. It is freely
available to us all. Be unconditional about
happiness and it will become
unconditional to you.

❖ ❖ ❖

64

There is no duty we so underrate as the duty of being happy. By being happy we sow anonymous benefits upon the world.

Robert Louis Stevenson, 1850–94

❖ ❖ ❖

65

A lazy summer's day by the beach is a
wonderful way to raise your spirits.

❖ ❖ ❖

66

Happiness: a good bank account, a good
cook, and a good digestion.

Jean-Jacques Rousseau, 1712–78

❖ ❖ ❖

67

The moon has a happy nature and it is the
same in any culture and in any language.
The man in the moon is always smiling.

❖ ❖ ❖

68

You can't chase happiness; it is not
something you pursue. This is because
happiness is not something outside you, it
is inside you. It is there already, all you
have to do is let it out.

❖ ❖ ❖

69

Sit quietly, doing nothing, spring comes,
and the grass grows by itself.

Zen saying

❖ ❖ ❖

70

There is no singular ingredient for
happiness, it can come from so many small
things or from one big event.

❖ ❖ ❖

71

Waking up on a summer morning to a
room filled with sunlight can bring you
happiness for the rest of the day.

✤ ✤ ✤

72

If you can spend a perfectly useless
afternoon in a perfectly useless manner,
you have learned how to live.

Lin Yutang, 1895 –1976

✤ ✤ ✤

73

You can get a warm feeling of happiness
and comfort from the smell of a
home-cooked meal as it drifts through the
house on a dark weekend afternoon.

❖ ❖ ❖

74

Being happy can be about choosing between resentment and joy. Resentment will restrain you in the past but joy will take you forward and free you from unhappiness.

❖ ❖ ❖

75

The discovery of a new dish does more for human happiness than the discovery of a new star.

Anthelme Brillat-Savarin, 1755–1826

❖ ❖ ❖

76

Good news delivers happiness, even more
so when it is unexpected.

77

Broaden your interests. The more interests
you have, the happier you will be.

❖ ❖ ❖

78

Any productive work you do will make a
positive contribution to the world. Keep
busy and keep happy.

❖ ❖ ❖

79

Your perception is important to happiness.
Happiness is nowhere and happiness is
now here are the same letters – they're
just read differently.

❖ ❖ ❖

80

You can gain happiness by relying on
yourself and by not being dependent on
others. Having control over your life can
be a source of serenity.

❖ ❖ ❖

81

People-watching can be a happy way to
spend an afternoon sitting in a cafe or
on a park bench.

❖ ❖ ❖

82

Be proud to just be yourself and generate
for yourself a sense of calmness,
relaxation and peace.

❖ ❖ ❖

83

True happiness, we are told, consists in getting out of one's self, but the point is not only to get out; you must stay out; and to stay out you must have some absorbing errand.

Henry James, 1843–1916

❖ ❖ ❖

84

Happiness can be achieved by finding inspiration in the ordinary and the everyday. For example, buds on trees after a long winter or sunlight after a heavy storm can motivate us onwards and upwards.

❖ ❖ ❖

85

Have a day where you're thankful for
everything. Say thank you for your
breakfast, thank you to the coffee,
to the house and garden. By seeing
the positive in everything you
will be much happier.

❖ ❖ ❖

86

My soul can find no staircase to heaven
unless it be through earth's loveliness.

Michelangelo, 1475–1564

✤ ✤ ✤

87

Remember all the things in the world
which are of importance to you.
Make a list of your friends, your favorite
places, your most enjoyable food, your
perfect holiday destination, your most
treasured memories.

✤ ✤ ✤

88

If you have a place to live and someone to love you are blessed.

Anon

89

A mild spring day when the birds come
home from migration will fill you
full of hope.

90

Happiness does not have to be earned or
deserved. The beauty of nature is free, a
smile is free, laughter and joy are free.

91

You are a king by your own fireside, as
much as any monarch on his throne.

Miguel de Cervantes Saavedra, 1547–1616

92

Some Buddhists believe that your
happiness is doubled every time you let
yourself be pleased for another person's
good fortune.

93

Happiness can come to you when you
turn a corner on a city street and stumble
upon a beautiful garden, window box
or sculpture.

94

Find ecstasy in life; the mere sense of
living is joy enough.

Emily Dickinson, 1830–86

❖ ❖ ❖

95

Smells can transport you to happy times
in your life. The smell of a rose garden
in midsummer, freshly brewed coffee
and the smell of bread baking are
universally comforting smells.

96

Happiness is like those palaces in fairy
tales whose gates are guarded by dragons:
we must fight in order to conquer it.

Alexander Dumas, 1824–95

❖ ❖ ❖

97

When you find something you think is
really great, you have found something
that makes you happy.

❖ ❖ ❖

98

To see a world in a grain of sand
And heaven in a wild flower
Hold infinity in the palm of your hand
And eternity in an hour.

William Blake, 1757–1827

❖ ❖ ❖

99

One happy person can have a huge
influence on the rest of the world.
Happiness is infectious and those touched
by it can catch it and spread it further.

❖ ❖ ❖

100

Happiness comes when your work and
words are of benefit to yourself and others.

Buddha, c. 400 BC

❖ ❖ ❖

101

Lambs in fields in the springtime are a
lovely reminder that the weather is getting
warmer and winter is nearly over.

❖ ❖ ❖

102

Instead of seeking joy, be joyful.
Instead of seeking love, be loving.
Instead of seeking peace, be peaceful.

❖   ❖   ❖

103

Happiness depends, as Nature shows,
Less on exterior things than most suppose.

William Cowper, 1731–1800

❖ ❖ ❖

104

There is no key to happiness. It is open
twenty-four hours a day and seven days a
week.

❖ ❖ ❖

105

Living a life of harmlessness to all living
beings brings happiness all around.

106

You cannot contain happiness nor control
it or keep it in. True happiness
is unselfish.

❖ ❖ ❖

107

Grief at the absence of a loved one is
happiness compared to life with a
person one hates.

Jean de la Bruyère, 1645–96

❖ ❖ ❖

108

Enjoy the moment, it can never be
too late to be happy.

109

Having someone to cook for you can bring
you a lot of pleasure.

❖ ❖ ❖

110

Being a friend to someone is a route
to your own happiness.

❖ ❖ ❖

111

The bills are paid, your in-tray in
empty and the sun is shining – a perfect
happy day.

❖ ❖ ❖

112

If you are too busy to be happy – you are
too busy being unhappy. Change your
outlook and your mood will change too.
Enjoy living in the moment doing what
you are doing.

❖ ❖ ❖

113

You can move yourself, change
your surroundings!

"For my part, I travel not to go anywhere,
but to go. I travel for travel's sake. The
great affair is to move."

Robert Louis Stevenson, 1850–94

114

You don't need to be angry or upset.
You can learn to forgive your enemies.
Forgiving someone can bring enormous
relief from anger and lead to
your happiness.

❖ ❖ ❖

115

Accept yourself and be free from the
judgements of other people.

❖ ❖ ❖

116

Imagine yourself walking along a beach
on a warm summer evening as the
sun is setting.

❖ ❖ ❖

117

Try to bring happiness to other people
and in this way you can bring happiness
to yourself too.

❖ ❖ ❖

118

Happiness is taking a moment to reflect
on the world and your place in it.

❖ ❖ ❖

119

The power of hope upon human exertion,
and happiness, is wonderful.

Abraham Lincoln, 1809–65

❖ ❖ ❖

120

Discovering mutual ground with someone
you thought was very different from you
can bring happiness to both of you.

❖   ❖   ❖

121

Happiness is like finding the sixpence in
the pudding. You are lucky to be here.

❖   ❖   ❖

122

Feeling grateful to someone who has
helped you can be a way of bringing more
happiness into your life.

❖   ❖   ❖

123

Keep being interested in the world, the
more interests you have the more likely
you are to be happy.

❖ ❖ ❖

124

Smile at people and they will usually smile
back. Smiling brings happiness.

❖ ❖ ❖

125

Plant a seed and think how you may have
started a forest which may be around for
thousands of years. Your actions here in
this life are important.

❖ ❖ ❖

126

Lovers who love truly do not write down
their happiness.

Anatole France, 1844–1924

❖ ❖ ❖

127

Happiness is about feeling safe,
loving and being loved.

❖ ❖ ❖

128

Go for a long walk then soak your feet in
warm water and daydream a little.

❖ ❖ ❖

129

Night-scented flowers on a summer
evening can bring you a glow of happiness.

✣ ✣ ✣

130

Happiness is reading a book without
any interruption.

✣ ✣ ✣

131

Express yourself. Having the freedom of
self-expression in your clothes,
house decorations and garden can
make you happy.

❖ ❖ ❖

132

There is only one passion, the passion
for happiness.

Denis Diderot, 1713–84

✤ ✤ ✤

133

Be loving and you will attract love.
Be friendly and you will attract friendships.
Be happy and you will attract happiness.

✤ ✤ ✤

134

Watching the imagination of children
playing can fill you with happiness.

❖ ❖ ❖

135

Learn to get rid of your fear and anxiety.
This way you will have more space
for happiness.

❖ ❖ ❖

136

Take a cool swim or shower on a hot
summer day.

❖ ❖ ❖

137

Happiness is about pleasing others.

❖ ❖ ❖

138

Believe that anything can happen and live
in a world of miracles.

❖ ❖ ❖

139

Hugs and kisses provide instant happiness.

❖ ❖ ❖

140

Make people in your life happy.

"The said truth is that it is the greatest happiness of the greatest number that is the measure of right and wrong."

Jeremy Bentham, 1748–1832

❖ ❖ ❖

141

Music is the perfect medicine for
unhappiness.

❖ ❖ ❖

142

Being happy does not mean you are
never sad. Happiness gives you the
ability to rid yourself of sadness.

❖ ❖ ❖

143

Have a long chat with an old friend
who knows you well and you will
relax and smile.

❖   ❖   ❖

144

Act to make positive changes to the world.
Don't minimize your contribution –
any activity can help change things
for the better.

❖ ❖ ❖

145

Health, learning and virtue will ensure
your happiness; they will give you a
quiet conscience, private esteem and
public honour.

Thomas Jefferson, 1743–1826

❖ ❖ ❖

146

Tell yourself that you will continue to be
happy as long as the sun rises in the
morning.

❖ ❖ ❖

147

Listen to the leaves in the wind as you
walk in the park or countryside.

❖ ❖ ❖

148

Have breakfast in bed and read the
Sunday papers.

❖ ❖ ❖

149

In theory there is a possibility of perfect happiness: to believe in the indestructible element within one, and not to strive towards it.

Franz Kafka, 1883–1924

❖ ❖ ❖

150

Think of life as a walk where you will make happy discoveries on the way.

❖ ❖ ❖

151

Happiness is found in the most
unlikely places, especially if you're not
looking for it.

✤   ✤   ✤

152

Spend some time singing and dancing and you will find it is a great release of tension.

❖ ❖ ❖

153

For an inward smile think of the expression on a child's face on Christmas morning.

❖ ❖ ❖

154

Cross a stream using stepping stones and
you get a smiling sense of achievement.

❖ ❖ ❖

155

Being creative can strengthen your enthusiasm in life and lead you to being happy. Creative people always find the world an interesting place full of ideas.

❖ ❖ ❖

156

Don't think of happiness as being solely dependent on success. You can have a good time trying.

❖ ❖ ❖

157

Be able to smile at yourself. This way
you will always have something to keep
you amused.

❖   ❖   ❖

InSite

158

Happiness is the meaning and the
purpose of life, the whole aim and end
of human existence.

Aristotle, 384–22 BC

✤ ✤ ✤

159

Listen to your footsteps as you walk
home from work or the shops.

✤ ✤ ✤

160

Being happy is hearing a mosquito and
remaining safely unbitten.

❖ ❖ ❖

161

Sit up talking all night with your
closest friends.

✤　✤　✤

162

Why go further and further,
Look, happiness is right here.
Learn how to grab hold of luck,
For luck is always there.

Johann Wolfgang von Goethe, 1749–1832

✤　✤　✤

163

Slow down a little and enjoy the life and
the people around you more.

164

Have warm bread or croissants for
breakfast with real butter and freshly
brewed hot coffee.

❖ ❖ ❖

165

Cultivate the ability to remain calm in all
circumstances regardless of difficulties.

❖ ❖ ❖

166

Conscious virtue is the only solid
foundation of all happiness; for riches,
power, rank, or whatever, in the common
acceptation of the word, is supposed to
constitute happiness, will never quiet,
much less cure, the inward pangs of guilt.

Philip Dormer Stanhope,
4th Earl of Chesterfield, 1694–1773

❖ ❖ ❖

167

Complete a difficult task and you will
feel happily satisfied.

✤ ✤ ✤

168

Enter into every endeavour vowing
to do your best.

✤ ✤ ✤

169

We find a delight in the beauty and
happiness of children that makes the
heart too big for the body.

Ralph Waldo Emerson, 1803–82

❖ ❖ ❖

170

Take comfort in how peaceful the
night can be.

✤ ✤ ✤

171

Imagine a lump of happiness.
Keep it, it is yours.

✤ ✤ ✤

172

Don't seek admiration or praise. You will
feel happiest when these are offered
without you looking for them.

❖ ❖ ❖

173

Know where you are going. No one is
unhappy when they know what they are
aiming for.

❖ ❖ ❖

174

Clear out your cupboards and send the
things you don't want to the charity
shop. The space left behind will
help you to feel calm.

❖ ❖ ❖

175

Recycle your garbage and know you are
contributing to a better, safer world.

❖   ❖   ❖

176

No matter what you look like on the outside nor how wealthy you are, your happiness is inside you.

"A face is too slight a foundation for happiness."

Mary Wortley, Lady Montagu, 1689–1762

❖ ❖ ❖

177

Go for a walk in the park and feed the
ducks and birds on a cold day. Their
gratitude will make you feel happy.

❖ ❖ ❖

178

Have a chat with a fellow traveller when
on a long train or plane journey. Showing
interest in someone else will confirm to
yourself that you are a good person.

❖ ❖ ❖

179

It is impossible to be interested and
depressed at the same time.

❖ ❖ ❖

180

The more you give to the moment in this life the more you will get out of the moment.

❖ ❖ ❖

181

Do not leave things unfinished or
unsaid. Tidiness leaves you feeling
liberated and happy.

❖ ❖ ❖

182

Make patterns with bare feet in wet sand –
they will be there long after you have
left the beach.

❖ ❖ ❖

183

The love of truth, virtue, and the
happiness of mankind are specious
pretexts, but not the inward principles
that set divines at work.

George Berkeley, 1685–1753

❖   ❖   ❖

184

Be generous today – generous people
attract friends and bring joy to themselves.

❖   ❖   ❖

185

Think of the smell of clean laundry
that has been dried outside on the
washing line.

❖   ❖   ❖

186

Decide to compliment the people you encounter today. Giving compliments will make you accept yourself as well as others.

❖ ❖ ❖

187

Find things that will expand your mind in a creative way. Creativity is a positive experience of the world.

❖ ❖ ❖

188

Remember all the happy surprises you have had in your life.

❖ ❖ ❖

189

Happiness is feeling relieved such as when a debt has been repaid, when someone you were worried about is safe or when a situation you were anxious about has turned out well.

❖　❖　❖

190

He who knows enough is enough, will always have enough

Lau-Tzu, c. 600 BC

❖ ❖ ❖

191

Be happy in the moment and stop wishing for a better past.

❖ ❖ ❖

192

You can defend yourself from a liar with
the truth and defend yourself from the
angry with love.

193

Don't be cynical – believe in
true happiness and you just might
experience it.

❖　❖　❖

194

Different men seek after happiness in
different ways and by different means, and
so make for themselves different modes of
life and forms of government.

Arisotle, 384–22 BC

❖　❖　❖

195

Learn to celebrate common everyday
events such as a coffee break
or dinner-time.

✣ ✣ ✣

196

The most simple of decisions such as to walk rather than use the car or to give to charity rather than ignore it can bring you happiness from the feeling that you are doing some good.

❖ ❖ ❖

197

Just be proud to be yourself and this could be your happiest discovery.

❖ ❖ ❖

198

Of the good things given between man
and woman,
I say that a neighbour true and loving in
heart to a neighbour
is a joy beyond all things else.

Pindar, 522–443 BC

199

Imagine you are smiling inwardly to
yourself no matter what circumstances you
find yourself in.

❖ ❖ ❖

200

A garden of daisies can be full of weeds
or full of flowers.

�֍   ✦   ✦

201

Happiness is always there inside you.
Forgive yourself and other people. Before
forgiveness comes in, think about how
other people hurt. This way you can see
yourself for what you actually are and not
how they want you to be. So finding
happiness is no longer rooted outside, but
it's inside you: what you see, how you
view things, what you want.

❖　❖　❖

202

Friendship is a strong and habitual
inclination in two persons to promote the
good and happiness of one another.

Eustace Budgell, 1686–1737

❖ ❖ ❖

203

Sometimes you can be happier not
conforming than by conforming to
the status quo.

❖　❖　❖

204

When you feel that justice has been
done you will experience greater peace
and happiness.

❖　❖　❖

205

Drop everything and you can
experience happiness.

❖ ❖ ❖

206

Silence accompanies the most significant expressions of happiness and unhappiness: those in love understand one another best when silent.

Anton Pavlovich Chekhov, 1860–1904

❖ ❖ ❖

207

Finding something that is so good that it exceeds the description will make a happy moment and a happy memory.

❖ ❖ ❖

208

Trying to ease the burden in somebody else's life will make you feel happier about yourself.

✿ ✿ ✿

209

A sunny day in the middle of winter will
do much to lift your spirits.

❖ ❖ ❖

210

You can be happy making music.
Whatever instrument you choose
(it could even be your voice), it's great
when you make the sound you wanted.

❖ ❖ ❖

211

Do a good deed and keep it to yourself.
It will give you a secret feeling
of happiness.

❖ ❖ ❖

212

To fill the hour, that is happiness; to fill
the hour, and leave no crevice for a
repentance or an approval. We live amid
surfaces, and the true art of life is to
skate well on them.

Ralph Waldo Emerson, 1803–82

❖ ❖ ❖

213

Looking out over a city at night is a very
special experience.

❖ ❖ ❖

214

Learn to receive blessings. Think of the
little things that make you happy or the
people who give you assurance when
you're good. Most of us have reasons
to be happy but we don't see them or
we take them for granted.

❖   ❖   ❖

215

Most of us have somebody to turn to.
Even in turmoil there are people who
will support you.

✤ ✤ ✤

216

A mother's happiness is like a beacon,
lighting up the future but reflected also on
the past in the guise of fond memories.

Honoré de Balzac, 1799–1850

✤ ✤ ✤

217

Take control of your time. Happy people
feel in control of their lives. Though we
often overestimate how much we can
accomplish in a day, we generally
underestimate how much we can
accomplish if we work on it bit by bit.

❖ ❖ ❖

218

O, how bitter a thing it is to look into happiness through another man's eyes!

William Shakespeare, 1564–1616

❖ ❖ ❖

219

Discover the best friend in you.
We can all change lives for the better.

❖ ❖ ❖

220

Keep the thought that when it rains –
at least it isn't snow.

221

Try counting the stars on a clear night.

❖ ❖ ❖

222

Be hopeful. Hoping is better than being optimistic because it's whole and real. Hopeful people always have something to look forward to.

❖ ❖ ❖

223

There are friendly people in the world if
you go out and look for them.

224

Going for a long drive in the country
is a lovely way to relax.

❖ ❖ ❖

225

Your children and grandchildren will have
their share of happiness; there's no need to
work like a horse for them.

Chinese proverb

❖ ❖ ❖

226

In the right frame of mind you can
actually enjoy crowds. They can feel
like a celebration.

227

All of Man's problems stem from his inability to sit quietly with himself.

Blaise Pascal, 1623–62

❖   ❖   ❖

228

Accept unhappiness. Allow yourself to go through unhappy times then choose to be happy.

❖   ❖   ❖

229

Try sitting in a big comfy chair with a
warm drink and a good book or film.

230

Happiness is the relief you feel after a
hot day when the night cools down
enough to sleep.

✣ ✣ ✣

231

Men who seek happiness are like
drunkards who can never find their house
but are sure that they have one.

Voltaire (François Marie Arouet),
1694–1778

✣ ✣ ✣

232

You can enjoy the rain. Try standing out
in it with your face to the sky.

❖　❖　❖

233

Remember, for every bit of road rage you
encounter there are people who actually do
know how to drive.

✢ ✢ ✢

234

Allow yourself to be warmed by the sun.

✢ ✢ ✢

235

People who are nice to you even when you don't speak their language make you feel positive and happy.

❖ ❖ ❖

236

Friends will make you happy. "Between
friends there is no need of justice."

Aristotle, 384–22 BC

❖ ❖ ❖

237

The moment when the sun breaks through
after the rain is always a happy moment.

❖ ❖ ❖

238

Take a moment to recollect your thoughts.
"When you go into the space of
nothingness, everything becomes known."

Buddha, c. 400 BC

239

Don't go on a walk – go on an adventure!

❖ ❖ ❖

240

Seeing someone again after they've
been away and you've really missed
them is a happy event.

❖ ❖ ❖

241

Don't hold on to negative thoughts
about yourself. Being happy means
letting them go.

❖ ❖ ❖

242

Waking up feeling really refreshed
makes for a happy day.

❖ ❖ ❖

243

It makes you happy when you receive a
thank you for helping somebody else.

❖ ❖ ❖

244

Have a soak in a bath full of bubbles and
see magic in the rainbow reflections on
the bubbles themselves.

❖   ❖   ❖

245

A happy thought attracts happy feelings.

❖ ❖ ❖

246

Happiness can be being in a situation
where you feel freedom to act as
you want to.

❖ ❖ ❖

247

Hope is itself a species of happiness,
and, perhaps, the chief happiness
which this world affords.

Samuel Johnson, 1709–84

❖ ❖ ❖

248

Thinking of the people who stay in touch
with you even when you are thousands of
miles away should brighten your day.

❖ ❖ ❖

249

Allow yourself to be inspired by love,
moved by beauty and guided by
knowledge.

❖ ❖ ❖

250

The secret of happiness is to admire
without desiring.

Francis Herbert Bradley, 1846–1924

❖ ❖ ❖

251

Happiness is beginning to understand
things you thought were baffling.

❖ ❖ ❖

252

The feeling you get when you have just
seen a shooting star.

❖ ❖ ❖

253

The wrapping can give you just as much
pleasure as the present itself.

254

Enduring happiness doesn't come from
success. Wealth is similar to health; the
utter absence of either one can breed
misery, but having them doesn't
guarantee happiness.

❖ ❖ ❖

255

Some cause happiness wherever they go;
others whenever they go.

Oscar Wilde, 1854–1900

❖ ❖ ❖

256

Act as if you're happy. Just by smiling, one can begin to feel better in the same way as scowling can result in feeling negative. Put on a happy face and see if you can trigger the happiness emotion.

❖ ❖ ❖

257

A good night's sleep. You can lead an active, vigorous life and reserve time for rejuvenating sleep and solitude.

❖   ❖   ❖

258

Nurture your closest relationships. Close, intimate friendships with those who care deeply about you can help you get through difficult times.

❖   ❖   ❖

259

You can vow to do the very best you
can in all that you do.

"The greatest danger for most of us is not
that our aim is too high and we miss it,
but that it is too low and we reach it."

Michelangelo, 1475–1564

260

Take time each day to pause and to reflect
on some positive aspect of one's life; such
as friends, family, health, freedom,
education, natural surroundings, and so
on. This increases the experience of
well-being and makes you happier.

❖ ❖ ❖

261

Happiness does not depend on
circumstances.

❖ ❖ ❖

262

Steps to Happiness

Everybody knows: You can't be all things
  to all people.
You can't do all things at once.
You can't do all things equally well.
You can't do all things better than
  everyone else.
Your humanity is showing just like
  everyone else's.
So:
You have to find out who you are, and be
  that.
You have to decide what comes first, and
  do that.
You have to discover your strengths, and
  use them.
You have to learn not to compete with
  others,
Because no one else is in the contest of
  being you.

Then:

You will have learned to accept your own
    uniqueness.

You will have learned to set priorities and
    make decisions.

You will have learned to live with your
    limitations.

You will have learned to give yourself the
    respect that is due.

And you'll be a most vital mortal.

Dare to believe:

That you are a wonderful, unique person.

That you are a once-in-all-history event.

That it's more than a right, it's your duty,
    to be who you are.

That life is not a problem to solve, but a
    gift to cherish.

And you'll be able to stay one up on what
    used to get you down.

Anon

❖ ❖ ❖

263

Happiness can be the moment you turn
off the light and snuggle down into bed
for a good night's sleep.

❖ ❖ ❖

264

You are just as important as anybody else.

❖ ❖ ❖

265

You can make people happy if you smile
when you talk.

❖ ❖ ❖

266

A moment when you realize you are
feeling happy but you can't think of the
reason why.

❖   ❖   ❖

267

The greatest happiness for the thinking person is to have explored the explorable and to venerate in equanimity that which cannot be explored.

Johann Wolfgang von Goethe 1749–1832

❖ ❖ ❖

268

Look at the world through your own unique eyes and make it yours.

❖ ❖ ❖

269

Pleasure comes from the outside,
happiness from the inside.

❖   ❖   ❖

270

In each of our lives there are two worlds.
One leads to a happy life and the other to
a life of frustration, despair and misery.
Choose to be happy.

❖ ❖ ❖

271

But does not happiness come from
the soul within?

Honoré de Balzac, 1799–1850

❖ ❖ ❖

272

Approach each new year with a
feeling of hope.

❖   ❖   ❖

Invite ✓

273

Focus beyond yourself and reach out to those in need. While happiness can increase helpfulness, doing good also makes one feel good.

❖ ❖ ❖

274

It is not the strongest of the species that survive, nor the most intelligent, but the one most responsive to change.

Charles Darwin, 1809–82

❖ ❖ ❖

275

Cheerfulness is contagious. Choose
cheerful people for your friends and
you become cheerful too.

❖ ❖ ❖

276

Fear less, hope more;
Whine less, breathe more;
Talk less, say more;
Hate less, love more;
And all good things are yours.

Swedish proverb

❖ ❖ ❖

277

You experience happiness after solving a
problem. You release your mind from
fears, worries and desires.

❖ ❖ ❖

278

The person who is a master in the art of living makes little distinction between their work and their play, their labor and their leisure, their mind and their body, their education and their recreation, their love and their religion. They hardly know which is which. They simply pursue their vision of excellence and grace in whatever they do, leaving others to decide whether they are working or playing. To them, they are always doing both.

Zen Buddhist

❖ ❖ ❖

279

Value people for what they are and not
what they have.

❖ ❖ ❖

280

Happiness is an important treasure –
unearth it and enjoy it.

❖ ❖ ❖

281

The excitement you feel when your
favourite author has written a new book.

❖ ❖ ❖

282

If you feel bored take a spontaneous expedition somewhere. You never know what you might find.

❖ ❖ ❖

283

Happiness means using your imagination. Create the world you want to live in.

❖ ❖ ❖

284

Doing nothing is happiness for children
and misery for old men.

Victor Hugo, 1802–85

❖   ❖   ❖

285

Go for a walk in the woods after it has
rained and smell the rich aroma of
damp earth.

❖ ❖ ❖

286

If you open yourself to others you will
discover mutual needs among your friends.

❖ ❖ ❖

287

You can be a source of kindness and
happiness for friends and family.

❖   ❖   ❖

288

No matter what race, culture or religion
we are, we can all realize happiness.

❖　❖　❖

289

The purpose of our lives is to be happy.

The 14th Dalai Lama

❖　❖　❖

290

When you can forgive the past you will
have a happy future.

❖   ❖   ❖

291

Sometimes when you look for something
amazing you actually find it.

❖   ❖   ❖

292

Acknowledge that things sometimes go
wrong and it won't necessarily spoil
your happiness.

❖   ❖   ❖

293

Try having a lazy day where you don't
actually have to do anything. If done
properly it will release you from stress
and rejuvenate your outlook.

294

Formula of my happiness: a Yes, a No,
a straight line, a goal.

Friedrich Nietzsche, 1844–1900

❖ ❖ ❖

295

Think of happiness as being like the
moon. When clouds obscure it,
it is still there.

❖ ❖ ❖

296

Happiness is getting home from work
after a busy and stressful day and
putting the kettle on.

❖ ❖ ❖

297

Make your favourite food and then
eat it with someone.

❖   ❖   ❖

298

When you are happy you are helping to
create a happier world.

❖   ❖   ❖

299

Happiness does not consist in things
themselves but in the relish we have of
them; and a man has attained it when he
enjoys what he loves and desires for
himself, and not what other people think
lovely and desirable.

François, duc de la Rochefoucauld, 1613–80

❖ ❖ ❖

300

Work on your self-confidence. Confident
people tend to be happier people.

❖ ❖ ❖

301

Know your values, never do anything
which conflicts with them and you will
know peace of mind.

❖ ❖ ❖

302

Give someone a hug. They will give it
back when you need it.

303

Happy the man whose wish and care
A few paternal acres bound
Content to breathe his naked air,
In his own ground.

Alexander Pope, 1688–1744

❖ ❖ ❖

304

Don't think about hate. We all have
happy memories, think of those instead.

❖ ❖ ❖

305

Keep a sense of curiosity about the world
and you will never be bored or unhappy.

306

You can spend the rest of your life in
happiness if you choose to.

❖ ❖ ❖

307

Cats are happiest when they are warm.
Snuggle up.

❖ ❖ ❖

308

To be perfectly happy it does not suffice
to possess happiness, it is necessary to
have deserved it.

Victor Hugo, 1802–85

❖ ❖ ❖

309

Go for a swim in the sea or a pool and
feel your muscles relax as the water
gently stretches them.

❖ ❖ ❖

310

It is a happy thought to know that
someone believes in you.

❖ ❖ ❖

311

Receiving happy news by post, phone,
email or word of mouth will always
cheer you up.

❖　❖　❖

312

One of the happiest things in the world is
going on a journey; but I like to go by
myself. I can enjoy society in a room;
but out of doors, nature is company
enough for me.

William Hazlitt, 1778–1830

❖ ❖ ❖

313

Try not to spend too much time thinking
about things that annoy you. Think of
things you like instead and they will
lighten your mood.

❖ ❖ ❖

314

If it is raining outside go out and let the
rain refresh your head. If it is snowing go
out and take a sleigh ride or build a
snowman. In the wind, go for a long
bracing walk. If it is sunny then lie in the
sun. There are no excuses.

❖ ❖ ❖

315

If you become determined to be happy
you will have fewer anxieties in your life.

❖ ❖ ❖

316

To be selfish, stupid and have good health
are three requirements for happiness,
though if stupidity is lacking all is lost.

Gustave Flaubert, 1821–80

❖ ❖ ❖

317

You can be determined to start being happy tomorrow.

❖ ❖ ❖

318

Go to a flea market, charity shop or junk shop and have a rummage for old treasures.

❖ ❖ ❖

319

Make a wish that may come true. Think of coincidences that have brought you happiness. You are laying the path to a happier world for yourself and others.

❖ ❖ ❖

320

Think of all the things you have in
common with your friends. They are
proof that you are loved.

❖ ❖ ❖

321

The smell of new paper in a book,
magazine or newspaper is a
feel-good smell.

❖ ❖ ❖

322

It is in the love of one's family only that
heartfelt happiness is known.

Thomas Jefferson, 1743–1826

❖ ❖ ❖

323

When you love someone, no distance
can keep you apart.

❖   ❖   ❖

324

Try opening up to the world today. You
can always retreat to solitude tomorrow.

❖ ❖ ❖

325

Happiness was not made to be boasted,
but enjoyed.

Thomas Traherne, 1636–74

❖ ❖ ❖

326

Beauty is everywhere and it doesn't
necessarily cost any money.

❖ ❖ ❖

327

You can help someone to discover their
own happiness without having to tell
them about your own.

✢ ✢ ✢

328

Buy someone a present and then
watch them unwrap it.

✢ ✢ ✢

329

Happiness does not notice the
passing of time.

Chinese proverb

❖ ❖ ❖

330

You can make someone else happy
just by being you.

✤ ✤ ✤

331

Happiness serves hardly any other purpose
than to make unhappiness possible.

Marcel Proust, 1871–1922

✤ ✤ ✤

332

Do not be afraid to be yourself or to
show your feelings to the world.

❖ ❖ ❖

333

Desire is happiness: satisfaction as
happiness is merely the ultimate moment
of desire. To be wish and wish
alone is happiness.

Friedrich Nietzsche, 1844–1900

❖ ❖ ❖

334

Use the telephone, there is always
someone's voice you'd love to hear.

❖ ❖ ❖

335

Rediscover your childlike excitement
of things.

❖　❖　❖

336

Being determined to be happy does not make you selfish or unkind. You have a right to be happy.

❖   ❖   ❖

337

When friends and family show you affection, be pleased with them and yourself for it.

❖   ❖   ❖

338

If it is a sunny day use it well and it will
give you happy memories.

❖   ❖   ❖

339

Happiness comes from our feelings and
not from things we can buy. We have
become so conditioned to seek happiness
indirectly that we do not always
understand the difference between
being happy for the short-term
and the long-term.

❖ ❖ ❖

340

In the midst of happiness, one may not
appreciate what happiness is.

Chinese proverb

❖   ❖   ❖

341

Always look on the happy side of life.
If you learn to laugh at life you will
feel better.

❖ ❖ ❖

342

Doing good is the greatest happiness.

Chinese proverb

❖ ❖ ❖

343

Cherish all your relationships, learn to
understand, not judge, your family
and friends.

❖ ❖ ❖

344

Learn to let go and trust yourself. Being
happy means learning to let go of
expectations from yourself or from
other people.

❖ ❖ ❖

345

Share yourself and help others.
Realizing that you're a good person
helps you to be happy.

❖ ❖ ❖

346

Be grateful. Develop in yourself the sense
of gratitude and be thankful for
what you have.

❖   ❖   ❖

347

Take responsibility for your life. We can
become very unhappy and very bitter
because we live blaming others for who we
are, where we're at, or how we should be.
It's an exhausting process because you'll
forever be blaming other people.

❖ ❖ ❖

348

A comfortable house is a great source of
happiness. It ranks immediately after
health and a good conscience.

Sydney Smith, 1771–1845

❖   ❖   ❖

349

Think of all the significant people in your
life. The reasons they are special are the
reasons you are special. Let this thought
make you happy.

❖ ❖ ❖

350

Shuffling through piles of fallen leaves in
autumn will reconnect you to the earth.

351

Don't look at things first with a critical eye. Try to look for joy and beauty first.

❖ ❖ ❖

352

Say thank you to someone who has recently done you a favour or shown kindness. It is impossible to be thankful and feel unhappy at the same time.

❖ ❖ ❖

353

I can be forced to live without happiness,
but I will never consent to live
without honor.

Pierre Corneille, 1606–84

354

Relax on a cold evening and stare into
the flames of a real fire.

❖ ❖ ❖

355

Go shopping and find a bargain in the
sales. Better still, find lots of bargains.

❖ ❖ ❖

356

Keep with you a sense that only good
can happen in the days to come.

357

Enjoy your achievements. Do not feel that
they are insignificant.

❖ ❖ ❖

358

The discovery of things that inspire us
can kindle happiness.

❖ ❖ ❖

359

Feel your feelings. You cannot be truly
happy and lie to yourself about
your sadness.

❖   ❖   ❖

360

To me it seems that to give happiness is a
far nobler goal that to attain it.

*Lewis Carroll (Charles Lutwidge Dodgson),
1832–98*

✤ ✤ ✤

361

Do not be afraid of being not good
enough. Just like the ugly duckling in the
fairy tale you will eventually find this is
not true.

✤ ✤ ✤

362

If you search for happiness it can be like a
cat chasing its tail. You go round and
round and still can't get to it. You must
choose happiness.

363

You can either remain tethered to land or
happily set sail on an ocean of discovery.

❖ ❖ ❖

364

Preparing for a holiday. Going on holiday.
Being on holiday. Bliss.

❖ ❖ ❖

365

We go to great pains to alter life for the happiness of our descendants and our descendants will say as usual: things used to be so much better, life today is worse than it used to be.

Anton Pavlovich Chekhov, 1860–1904